P9-DVU-192

POP CULTURE BIOS

EMMA WATSON

FROM WIZARDS TO WALLFLOWERS

NADIA HIGGINS

Lerner Publications Company
MINNEAPOLIS

Lerner Publications Company
A division of Lerner Publishing Group, Inc.
241 First Avenue North
Minneapolis, MN 55401 U.S.A.

For reading levels and more information, look up this title at www.lernerbooks.com.

Library of Congress Cataloging-in-Publication Data

Higgins, Nadia.
Emma Watson : from wizards to wallflowers / by Nadia Higgins.
pages cm. — (Pop culture bios)
Includes index.
ISBN 978-1-4677-1442-6 (lib. bdg. : alk. paper)
ISBN 978-1-4677-2499-9 (eBook)
1. Watson, Emma, 1990- —Juvenile literature. 2. Actors—Great Britain—Biography—Juvenile literature. I. Title.
PN2598.W25H54 2014
791.4302'8092—dc23 [B] 2013019754

Manufactured in the United States of America
1 – PC – 12/31/13

INTRODUCTION

Emma celebrates the opening of *Harry Potter and the Deathly Hallows: Part 2* with costars (LEFT TO RIGHT) Alan Rickman, Tom Felton, Daniel Radcliffe, Rupert Grint, and Matthew Lewis.

WORLD PREMIERE = the first showing of a work of art, such as a movie

For years, reporters have been asking Emma Watson about this day. What will it feel like? How will she cope? It's July 7, 2011—the day of Emma's last-ever Harry Potter world premiere. *Harry Potter and the Deathly Hallows: Part 2* is about to cap off the top-earning movie series of all time.

Emma has spent more than half her life playing Hermione. And now, at the end of it all, **it's "so overwhelming,"** Emma says.

Emma looked gorgeous in her ruffled dress at the world premiere of *Harry Potter and the Deathly Hallows: Part 2* in London.

Emma dons her finest for a special event in New York.

Huge banners featuring her face flutter in London's Trafalgar Square. Thousands of fans fill the plaza. Emma steps out onto an enormous red carpet. "Emma! Emma!" the crowd screams. A tangle of arms reaches for her.

Finally, Emma's onstage giving her thank-you speech. As she starts naming the people she's worked with, her voice chokes. "That's it. I'm gone!" she says, half crying, half laughing.

But she carries on. **"I'm so proud to have been a part of this,"** she states. She says it's been "a privilege" to play such a strong female character.

But Emma will soon be filming her first major role since Harry Potter. She's slated to play Sam in *The Perks of Being a Wallflower*. After ten-plus years as Hermione, she is scared and excited to try a new part. This emotional day has been one of good-byes. But it also marks a new beginning in Emma's busy, creative life.

Emma laughs on and off set with *Perks* costars Logan Lerman (LEFT) and Ezra Miller (CENTER).

CHAPTER ONE

PRIMED FOR SUCCESS

Emma and her brother Alex (LEFT) attended the L.A. premiere of *Harry Potter and the Order of the Phoenix* together.

Glamorous, witty, and talented—to Emma Watson's fans, she is all of these things and more. But the British actress and model is also known for being reserved and seriously brainy. Since the age of seven, she's wavered between wanting to be an actress and wanting to be a student. All in all, Em has loved the adventure of finding her way. How did it all begin?

A Big Family

Emma's parents, Chris Watson and Jacqueline Luesby, are both British. But Emma's father has French roots. In 1990, the couple was living in Paris, France. On April 15, they welcomed Emma Charlotte Duerre Watson into their lives. Three years later, Emma's brother Alex was born.

EMMA BASICS

NICKNAME: Em
HEIGHT: 5 feet 5 inches (1.7 meters)
PETS: two cats and a dog
BAD HABIT: keeping the heat too high
TO-DO LIST: get better at French
CAR: Toyota Prius

When Emma was five, her parents divorced. Everybody moved back to England, and her mother soon married again. Emma and Alex would live with their mother, stepfather, and two stepbrothers. The two siblings would spend weekends with their dad.

Emma's father would also remarry and have three more children. By the age of fourteen, Emma would be the oldest of seven. These days, Emma speaks fondly of her big, complicated family. Her parents' split was friendly, she says. She is close to both of them.

A Top-Notch School

Both of Emma's parents are lawyers. Growing up, Emma soaked in an atmosphere of books and learning. Watching movies was a rare treat.

SIB STORY

Emma's brother Alex has been her date at tons of Harry Potter events. Alex is a model, and the two sibs have also done photo shoots together. Emma's half sisters, Nina and Lucy, are twins born in 2004. In 2007, Lucy played a younger Emma in the made-for-TV movie *Ballet Shoes*.

SHE CAN PUNT

Emma was pretty outdoorsy when she was younger. She loved to spend the day doing what the Brits call punting. That's where you power a boat down a river by pushing a pole against the river bottom. Sometimes Emma would get attacked by swans!

Emma says her parents were strict. Well into her Hermione years, Emma had to do daily chores. At restaurants, she was not allowed to order off the kids' menu. Her parents expected her to try a wide variety of foods, rather than eating only burgers, pizza, and other kid-friendly meals.

Emma went to an expensive private school in Oxford. At the age of seven, she entered a contest to recite a poem. That's when she fell in love with acting. **"I loved finding out the real meaning of all the words, and how I could say them, and what I could do with my voice,"** she reflected in an interview with *Marie Claire*.

Soon the straight-A student was playing the lead in school plays. And her teachers were taking note of her talent.

RECITE = to say from memory

When she tried out for Hermione, Emma had no idea how popular she would become.

One of Thousands

In 1999, casting directors started a huge search to find the stars of the first Harry Potter movie. They visited hundreds of schools across England. In the end, they would audition forty thousand children for the roles of Harry, Ron, and Hermione.

Emma's teachers chose a group of about twenty kids to present to the directors. Emma was sent to the school gym and had her picture taken. Three weeks later, she got a call. Would she like to try out for Hermione? Emma was already a huge Potter fan. She wanted—needed—to get that role.

CASTING DIRECTORS = movie professionals in charge of hiring actors

Over the coming months, she would be called back eight times for follow-up tryouts. Emma showed how determined she could be. One day, she practiced the same lines for eight hours straight.

At auditions, Emma showed her acting chops. She also answered tons of personal questions. The directors wanted to make sure she could handle the hard work ahead. In August 1999, they announced their decision. Emma Watson was primed to become one of the most famous kids on the planet.

Emma, Rupert Grint (RIGHT), and Daniel Radcliffe (CENTER) became friends right away!

Emma spent years filming the Harry Potter movies at the studio in Leavesden, near London.

CHAPTER TWO
GROWING UP ON-SCREEN

Daniel Radcliffe (CENTER) and Emma (RIGHT) show up at MTV's *Total Request Live* (*TRL*) with fans.

The Harry Potter movies were shot in an old airport factory outside of London. The studio was its own magical world. It had an orchard out back, where Emma liked to hide. Wizards and witches filled the hallways and cafeteria. Emma's favorite place was the makeup trailer. She would get lost for hours playing with lipsticks and powders.

Staying Grounded

Hollywood has plenty of sad stories of childhood stars. Too often, they grow up too fast and lose their way. But the adults in Emma's life protected her from that fate. They treated her like a regular kid.

SHE'S BEEN THERE

Emma doesn't share the deets of her love life. She has fessed up to one epic crush, though. Between the ages of ten and twelve, Emma was head over heels for actor Tom Felton (Draco Malfoy). Poor Em, though. Tom only saw her as a little sis. "It was gutting, really," says Em.

Tom Felton—Emma's grade-school crush

Plus, Daniel Radcliffe (Harry) and Rupert Grint (Ron) were with her every step of the way. They were like brothers. They teased her all the time. But Rupert never failed to cheer her up. Daniel was her rock when she needed to pour her heart out.

Crazy Days

Emma worked eleven months out of every year. The studio was a two-hour drive away. She'd wake up at six and come home at nine each night. At the studio, she split her time filming and working with a tutor.

EMMA WATSON, POTTERHEAD

EMMA'S FAVORITE HP BOOK: *Harry Potter and the Prisoner of Azkaban*

WHICH MAGICAL ITEM EMMA WISHES SHE HAD: Hermione's time turner

WHICH MAGICAL CREATURE SHE'D BE: a mermaid

WHO SHE'D LIKE TO PLAY MOST BESIDES HERMIONE: Draco Malfoy

HARDEST SCENES TO FILM: kissing Rupert and Daniel

Emma became a great actress, but she also wanted to be a normal teenager.

Emma could feel herself getting better as an actress. Doing stunts and working with animals was also a blast. Still, Emma missed her family. She missed school. Going to a birthday party or a sleepover was out of the question.

Meanwhile, the Harry Potter movies kept coming out. Emma's fame blew her mind. She'd see her face everywhere: on billboards, on pencil cases, and even on Lego sets. Emma got mobbed in public. She found herself running out of restaurants or hiding out in stores. She had to give up riding the bus in her hometown.

Creeping Doubts

By 2007, Emma started to feel trapped. She hated the feeling of people watching her every move. Plus, the brainy teen had so many passions she wanted to explore. Did she even want to be an actress anymore?

After the fifth movie, Emma held off renewing her contract. But in the end, she realized she wouldn't be able to bear seeing Hermione played by someone else. She worked out a deal with the movie studio. She would stay on *if* they would allow time for her to go to college. What could they do but say yes?

CONTRACT = a legal agreement, often about the terms of a job

KA-CHING!

In 2010, Emma was named the highest-paid actress in Hollywood. She had earned $15 million each for the two *Deathly Hallows* movies. By 2012, she was sitting on a $40 million fortune.

Looking back, Emma's so glad she didn't walk away. She loves the dark energy of the last three Harry Potter films. Also, she got the chance to see Hermione blossom as a feminist. Was it weird to grow up on-screen? No doubt. Still, Emma says she **"wouldn't swap it in a million years."**

FEMINIST = a person who fights for women's rights

Emma giggles on the red carpet, on her way to the London premiere of *Harry Potter and the Deathly Hallows: Part 2.*

Dame Vivienne Westwood (LEFT) presents the award for Style Icon to Emma at the 2011 ELLE Style Awards.

CHAPTER THREE

THE PERKS OF BEING EMMA

Emma wore Chanel (LEFT) for the premiere of *The Bling Ring*. A model (RIGHT) shows off a favorite quote of People Tree—a clothing company which featured Emma's designs—while wearing one of the company's spring/summer outfits.

Back when Emma was around fourteen, the clothing maker Chanel had started loaning her clothes. Even then, word was spreading about Emma's awesome style. Chanel knew that having Emma seen in its clothes was good for business.

In 2009, Emma became a model for Burberry, another high-fashion clothing brand. She also started designing her own line for People Tree. This fair trade clothing company is close to Emma's heart.

Emma sparkles in a Burberry dress.

FAIR TRADE = made by workers in poor countries who are paid well

Some clothing factories in poor countries treat workers like slaves. People Tree pays workers in poor countries a fair wage.

Emma's cute tanks and dresses were especially for teens. She believed young people deserved to feel good about the way their clothes are made.

Emma's Faves

- Food: baked beans on toast
- Color: white or cream
- Night out: dancing to live music
- Way to relax: soaking in the tub
- Sports: field hockey, table tennis
- Hobby: painting

Off to School

That fall, Emma's life turned in yet another direction. She headed off to Brown University in Providence, Rhode Island. All she wanted was to be a normal college student. Would her classmates be cool with that?

As it turned out—yes! At last, Emma was just one of the crowd.

Emma's Peeves

- Being called Emily Watson
- Guys in flip-flops
- The silent treatment
- Bad manners
- Grumpy cabdrivers

GREAT HAIR DAYS

In June 2010, filming for Harry Potter wrapped. Emma was free to do something she'd wanted to do for years. She got a pixie cut! Not everybody loved it, but Emma did. "I've never felt so confident as I did with short hair," she spilled to *Glamour*.

She lived in a dorm with five other women. She went to parties. She wore the few comfy clothes that fit in her small closet.

At first, Emma wasn't sure what she wanted to major in. (She later chose English.) But right away, the world-famous actress signed up for . . . acting classes. She'd been playing Hermione for so long. She wondered if she had the skills to play other people.

On to *Perks*

In the fall of 2010, Emma was a busy college sophomore. She was still open to shooting films during breaks, though. She asked her agent to pass along only the *very* best scripts.

AGENT = a person who finds parts for actors

Emma sobbed as she read *The Perks of Being a Wallflower* script. This gritty story about a group of high school friends was so amazing. She wanted to run out and share it with the world! That's how she knew she needed to play Sam.

Emma would have to beat a serious case of nerves, though. Sam was such a free spirit. In one scene, she does a funny-sexy dance in a skimpy corset. That made Emma

Emma got to embrace her wild side in the role of Sam for *The Perks of Being a Wallflower.*

CORSET =

an old-fashioned undergarment that squeezes a woman around her middle

squirm. Then there was the American accent. And she didn't know anything about high school life.

Emma sent an e-mail to the director. He could find someone better than her for the part, she wrote. He told her to stop worrying about "external" things. He thought she was perfect for the role!

Emma started preparing to play Sam. She wrote in a diary as if she were Sam. She listened to Sam's favorite band, the Smiths, over and over. She worked with a voice coach to nail the American accent.

Perks filmed in the summer of 2011 in Pittsburgh, Pennsylvania. Emma had the time of her life!

Pittsburgh, Pennsylvania, was the setting for *The Perks of Being a Wallflower* film.

Emma had a blast with *Perks* costars Logan Lerman (CENTER) and Ezra Miller (RIGHT).

The whole cast lived together in a hotel. Every night, they ate together and played games. Emma was the singer in a band with costars Logan Lerman and Ezra Miller. They called themselves Octopus Jam and rocked out late into the night.

A Lifelong Learner

Perks proved to the world—and to Emma—that she had plenty of talent. It also made Emma realize that she really did want to be an actress. In the summer of 2012, she filmed *The Bling Ring*. This time, she played a teen who robs celebrities' homes.

Soon after, Emma headed to Iceland to film *Noah*. She was slated to play a daughter of the famous biblical figure. The cast included some big names, such as Russell Crowe. Emma felt a little intimidated!

Luckily, her *Perks* costar Logan Lerman was also on set. Their very first scene was together. Emma relied on her good friend and Octopus Jam bandmate to break the ice.

Emma has been so busy making movies. She's had to take some breaks from college to get it all done. But she still plans to nab that English degree. Knowing Emma, she'll find a way!

What's next for Emma Watson? She'll keep looking for scripts that make her want to share them with the world. She'll choose roles that challenge her. She'll find directors who can teach her. As Emma put it, **"I have so much to learn, and I couldn't be more excited about that."**

ASK EMMA

ON PRIORITIES: "Friends and family come first and work comes second; that's just how I live my life."

ON FASHION: "I wear . . . what I feel comfortable wearing. I care but not hugely."

ON SUCCESS: "If you truly pour your heart into what you believe in, even if it makes you vulnerable, amazing things will happen."

EMMA PICS!

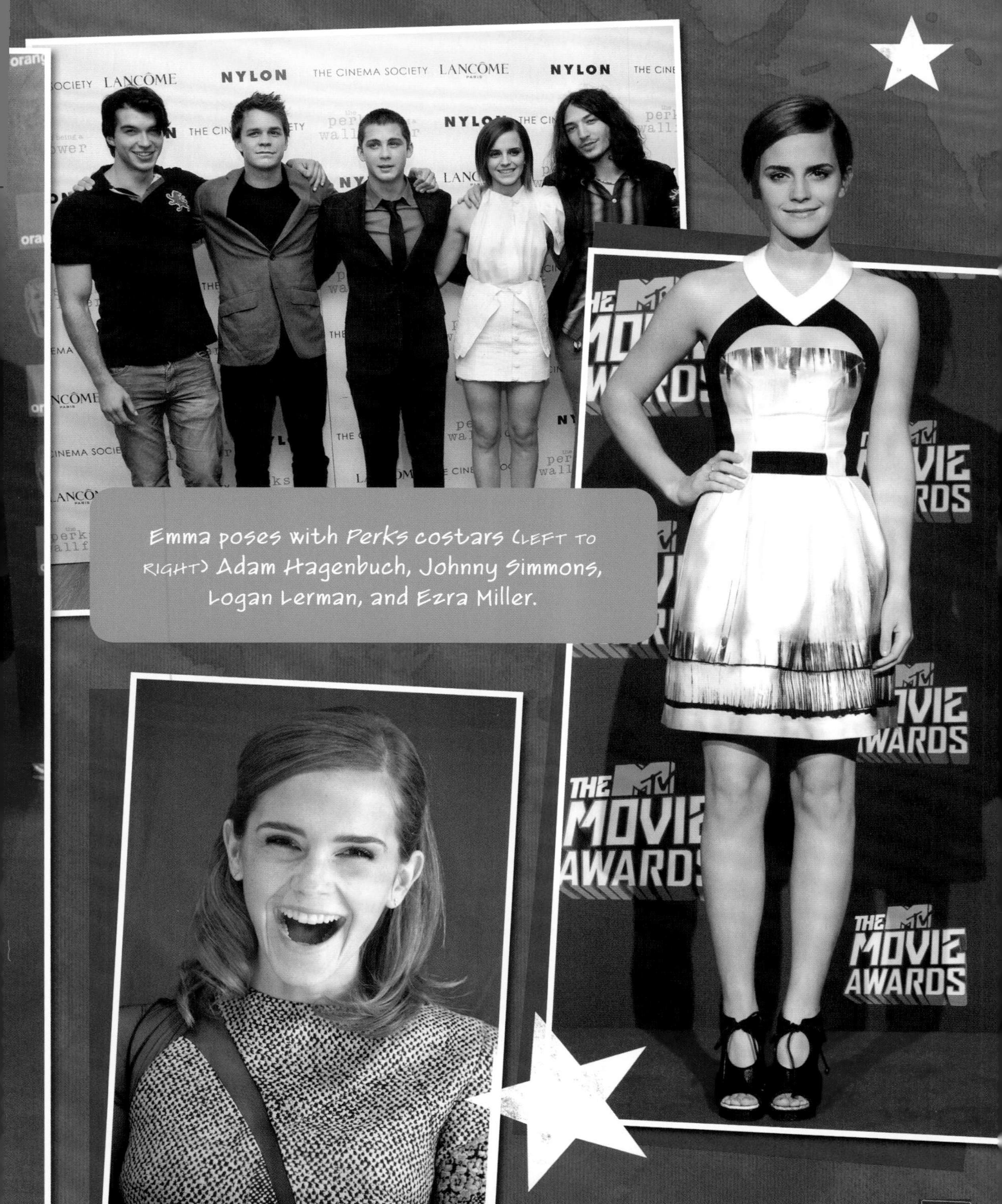

Emma poses with *Perks* costars (LEFT TO RIGHT) Adam Hagenbuch, Johnny Simmons, Logan Lerman, and Ezra Miller.

SOURCE NOTES

5. "Emma Watson Interview at Last Ever Harry Potter World Premiere," YouTube video, 2:27, posted by Absolute Radio, July 7, 2011, http://www.youtube.com/watch?v=cyDhVB8a97U.
7. "Emma Watson's Thank You Speech—*Deathly Hallows* Pt 2 World Premiere," YouTube video, 2:05, posted by Andrew Griffin, July 8, 2011, http://www.youtube.com/watch?v=oLLRknEIsGU.
11. Alison Edmond, "Enchanting Emma," *Marie Claire*, December 2010, 156.
15. "*The Jonathan Ross Show*—Emma Watson Interview," YouTube video, 12:20, posted by BritanniaOne, January 20, 2013, http://www.youtube.com/watch?v=8D8JavtD6TE.
19. Emma Watson, *Woman's Hour*. BBC, podcast, December 15, 2008, http://www.bbc.co.uk/radio4/womanshour/01/2008_51_mon.shtml.
23. Emma Rosenblum, "Emma Watson Talks Style, Dating, and Life after Harry Potter in Her October 2012 *Glamour* Interview," *Glamour*, September 4, 2012, http://www.glamour.com/entertainment/blogs/obsessed/2012/09/emma-watson-talks-style-dating.html.
25. "Q & A with Emma Watson," *Savoir Flair*, November 4, 2012, http://savoirflair.com/magazine/interview-emma-watson.
27. Jeff Jensen, "The Story of Emma Watson," *Entertainment Weekly*, July 8, 2011, 62.
27. Kaitlin Cubria, "Emma Watson Admits: 'I'm a Bit OCD about Perfectionism' to 'Marie Claire,'" *Teen.com*, January 4, 2013, http://www.teen.com/2013/01/04/celebrities/celebrity-quotes/emma-watson-marie-claire-uk-february-2013-cover/.
27. Jadi Bryson, "Emma . . . Hermione . . . Same Girl?," *Girls' Life*, December 2005, 48.
27. "Emma Watson Accepts the Award for MTV Trailblazer," MTV video, 2:38, April 14, 2013, http://www.mtv.com/videos/misc/898736/emma-watson-accepts-the-award-for-mtv-trailblazer.jhtml#id=1704844.

MORE EMMA INFO

Emma's Facebook Page
https://www.facebook.com/emmawatson
Check here for updates straight from Em.

Higgins, Nadia. *Logan Lerman: The Perks of Being an Action Star*. Minneapolis: Lerner Publications, 2014. Get the inside scoop on Emma's *Perks* costar and Octopus Jam bandmate.

People: Emma Watson
http://www.people.com/people/emma_watson
The editors of *People* magazine put together a nice snapshot of Em's life, including a great timeline.

Sibley, Brian. *Harry Potter Film Wizardry*. New York: HarperCollins, 2012. Get all the behind-the-scenes info on how the Harry Potter movies were made.

Teen.com: Emma Watson
http://www.teen.com/tag/emma-watson
This site hosts some pretty off-the-wall vids of Emma. See her talk about her gross first kiss and more.

INDEX

PHOTO ACKNOWLEDGMENTS

The images in this book are used with the permission of: © Mark Cutherbert/UK Press/Getty Images, p. 2; © Photo by Jim Smeal/WireImage/Ron Galella Collection/Getty Images, p. 3 (top); © Vera Anderson/WireImage/Getty Images, pp. 3 (bottom), 29 (bottom left); © Jim Spellman/WireImage/Getty Images, pp. 4 (top left), 6, 9; © Mike Marsland/WireImage/Getty Images, p. 4 (top right); © D. Dipasupil/FilmMagic/Getty Images, p. 4 (bottom); © Featureflash/Dreamstime.com, pp. 5, 28 (bottom left); Summit Entertainment/The Kobal Collection, pp. 7, 26; © Justin Goff/UK Press/Getty Images, p. 8 (top); © Lisa C'Connor/ZUMA Press/Alamy, p. 8 (bottom); © Presselect/Alamy, p. 10; © Grant Faint/Getty Images, p. 11; © Nicolas Asfouri/AFP/Getty Images, p. 12; © Dave Hogan/Hulton Archive/Getty Images, p. 13; © Ian Macpherson/Alamy, p. 14 (top left); © Jim Smeal/WireImage/Ron Galella/Getty Images, p. 14 (top right); © Theo Wargo/WireImage/Getty Images, p. 14 (bottom); © Joe Seer/Shutterstock.com, pp. 15, 27; © Andrew Fox/Terra/CORBIS, p. 16; © Anthony Jones/Mark Cuthbert/UK Press/Getty Images, p. 17; © Mark Cutherbert/UK Press/Getty Images, p. 18; © Christopher Pledger /eyevine/Redux, p. 19; © Ian Gavan/Getty Images, p. 20 (top); © Jason LaVeris/FilmMagic/Getty Images, p. 20 (bottom left); © Camera Press/Redux, p. 20 (bottom right); © Getty Images for Burberry, p. 21; © St. Clair/Macpherson/Splash News/CORBIS, p. 22; © Andrew Cowie/Redux, p. 23; © Glenn Weiner/ZUMAPRESS/ImageCollect, p. 24; © R. Gino Santa Maria/Dreamstime.com, p. 25; © Dave Hogan/Getty Images, p. 28 (right); © Frederick Injimbert/ZUMAPRESS.com/ImageCollect, p. 28 (top left); © Stephen Lovenkin/Getty Images, p. 29 (top left); Picture Perfect/Rex USA, p. 29 (right).

Front cover: © Kevan Brooks/AdMedia (main); © Henry Harris/Featureflash/ImageCollect (inset).

Back cover: © Frederick Injimbert/ZUMAPRESS.com/ImageCollect.

Main body text set in Shannon Std Book 12/18.
Typeface provided by Monotype Typography.